THE HIEROGLYPHS HANDBOOK

PHILIP ARDAGH

faber and faber

First published in 1999
by Faber and Faber Limited
3 Queen Square, London WC1N 3AU

Printed in Italy

Page layout: Mackerel

A CIP record for this book
is available from the British Library

ISBN 0 -571-19744 -2

2 4 6 8 10 9 7 5 3 1

THE HIEROGLYPHS HANDBOOK

Philip Ardagh has written around forty books,
under a variety of names, including a number on
Ancient Egypt. He writes everything from histories
to horror stories – that's just the 'h's – and his
books have been translated into nine different
languages (10, if you count Latin).
He lives with a wife and two cats in a seaside town
in England, and loves walking along the beach,
and combing his beard (though not neccessarily at
the same time).

To Heloise, my wife,
Martin, my brother,
and
Ra, the mighty sun god & dung beetle.

CONTENTS

"WAKE ME UP WHEN
HE'S FINISHED."

A MESSAGE FROM THE AUTHOR

I t took the average Ancient Egyptian scribe about twelve years to learn all the hieroglyphs he'd need to get through his writing career without having to make up squiggles of his own (and hope that no-one would notice).

Even if you read this book v-e-r-y s-l-o-w-l-y it won't take you that long, which should give you a clue as to what I'm going to say next. What this book certainly WON'T do is make you an internationally famous world expert on Ancient Egyptian hieroglyphs.

What it *should* do is give you a good idea of the basics and get you started reading and writing your own messages in Ancient Egyptian, which is very satisfying and (excellent) fun.

"I GIVE UP!
I CAN'T GET A
MOMENT'S PEACE
AROUND HERE!"

A_{NOTHER} MESSAGE FROM THE AUTHOR

This is the part where I get to thank all the people who helped to make this book possible. Let me start with my editor, Suzy, who can now add editing hieroglyphic text to her many publishing skills. Thanks, Suzy.

Because the only Ancient Egyptians around today are mummified and usually in museums, I had to turn to modern experts for help and advice when writing this book. Very wisely, they seem to wish to remain anonymous – some of them even took early retirement. Many thanks to them too. The expertise is theirs. Any mistakes are, of course, mine... or Suzy's. (Probably Suzy's.) A special thanks to Delia Pemberton, visiting lecturer at the British Museum, for casting her beady eye over everything before it went off to the printers.

This book is jam-packed full of hieroglyphs. There are examples of them everywhere. They're even in the chapter headings and cartoons.

You probably won't be able to draw them exactly as they look on the page, but the more you practise the better you'll be.

You'll find some of the more frequently used glyphs – that's what the little picture symbols are called – have been printed good and large in the back of the book, so you can trace them if you want to – but your best bet is to have a pen and paper handy as you read. That way you can practise drawing the glyphs that interest you. There are quizzes to answer along the way, to see just how good a scribe you'll turn out to be.

Pretty soon, you'll be reading and writing in hieroglyphs on your own!

"SIR! I HAVEN'T DONE MY HOMEWORK BECAUSE NOBODY'S INVENTED WRITING YET!"

A FEW WORDS ABOUT WORDS

Writing is a kind of code, so what you're doing right now is decoding. Because you've learnt to crack this code – by learning to read English – the words on the page make sense to you. It seems easy, but an Ancient Egyptian would probably have given up already, muttering something about 'meaningless squiggles' and having to 'go and build a pyramid'.*

"BOTHER! I MUST HAVE READ THESE INSTRUCTIONS THE WRONG WAY UP."

It's worth remembering that people were speaking long before anyone came up with the idea of writing. First came people, then came grunts, then speech, then finally writing. And writing really was a long, long way behind – about 94,500 years after the first 'true' humans came blinking into the world.

*Most Ancient Egyptians couldn't read Ancient Egyptian either.

These first true humans – called *Homo sapiens sapiens* by the experts, but probably 'Ugh', 'Huh' and 'Erh' by each other – were walking on this Earth about 100,000 years ago. But people didn't start writing until about 5,500 years ago, which is where the gap of about 94,500 years comes in. (For any Ancient Egyptians reading this, that number is 𓏏𓏏𓏏𓏏𓏏𓏏𓏏𓏏𓏏𓏏𓏏𓏏𓏏𓏏.)

The day people started writing things down is the day humankind officially stepped from the prehistoric era into history, though they didn't know this at the time, of course.

ANCIENT EGYPTIAN

The language of the Ancient Egyptians is one of the oldest on Earth. It was spoken from about 4000 BC – that's nearly 6,000 years ago – right up until the 11th century AD, but it wasn't always spoken or written down in the same way.

HIEROGLYPHS

The earliest Ancient Egyptian writing was the hieroglyphic script.

Hieroglyphs are what most of us think of when we talk about Ancient Egyptian writing. It's the picture writing you'll find on the walls of pharaohs' tombs, carved into ancient temple columns or written on the mummy cases of the dead. It's a useful language to be able to read if you're trying to avoid three-thousand-year-old curses, or trying to find out who's buried in that sarcophagus you smuggled out of a museum.

These Ancient Egyptian hieroglyphs spell out a single word of warning:

BEWARE

When writing with hieroglyphs, there's no punctuation to worry about – no full stops, commas, question marks, or anything like that. This makes it easier to write... but much harder to read, especially when there are no gaps between the words either!

You can find out more about the development of the very idea of 'writing' itself later, on page 78 of *The Hieroglyphs Handbook*. In the meantime, though, let's...

"HI THERE! DON'T WORRY. THEY WON'T BITE. I'VE JUST FED THEM."

...MEET THE GLYPHS

In the beginning, the glyph of an owl meant an owl. Nothing more and nothing less. This was fine if you wanted to write about owls – or something equally easy to draw – but not so useful when it came to trying to write about things such as love or hunger, or not liking your sister.

These most straightforward and basic glyphs are called 'ideograms' by some experts and 'logograms' by others. They represent objects or actions.

This glyph of a duck started life as an ideogram, simply meaning 'duck'.

This ideogram of a pair of legs doesn't mean 'legs' but the action, 'to walk' or 'to run'.

This ideogram, of a man with his hands tied behind his back, can mean either 'foreigner' or 'enemy', which shows what Ancient Egyptians thought of non-Egyptians!

Over time, 'sound' glyphs developed. These symbols represented sounds which, when spoken together, made up words. Language experts have given this approach to writing an important sounding name – the *rebus principle* – but it's really very straightforward.

In English, it would be like writing pictures of a bee and of a leaf. Put the two together and you get the word 'belief'. The final word is nothing to do with bees or leaves, but the pictures 'sound out' the word for you.

'bee' + 'leaf' = 'belief'

The 'belief' example of the rebus principle is the one you'll find in most books because it's such a good one.

Sound glyphs are called phonograms and, as with the English 'bee leaf' example, what a phonogram looks like and what it means are two totally separate things.

13

As an ideogram, this glyph simply means 'duck'. As a phonogram, it means the word 'son' (because the two words sounded very similar in Ancient Egyptian).

THE ALPHABET

There are probably over 6,000 different Ancient Egyptian glyphs in all, but a certain group of phonograms (sound glyphs) were used far more often than any others, and appear time and time again. There are twenty four of them and, to make life simple, they're often referred to as the Ancient Egyptian alphabet.

So that Egyptologists (experts on Ancient Egyptian) can speak the words created in hieroglyphs, these glyphs have been given sound values – in other words, it's been agreed how they should be pronounced. But, remember, there's no real way of knowing how an Ancient Egyptian would have actually pronounced them thousands of years ago.

    'to speak'   'to hear'

THE CORE ALPHABET

GLYPH	PICTURE	PRONUNCIATION
	vulture	ah
	reed leaf	i (as in pen and ink)
	arm	a (as in apple)
	quail chick	u, w
	leg	b (as in bunion)
	reed stool or mat	p (as in petal)
	horned viper	f (as in frightening)
	owl	m (as in moon)
	mouth	r (as in grin)
	water	n
	courtyard or shelter	h (soft 'h' as in hut)
	twisted rope	h (hard 'h' as in hack)
	sieve	kh (soft 'kh' as in Loch Ness)
	animal's belly	kh (hard 'kh')
	door bolt	z
	folded cloth	s

15

GLYPH	PICTURE	PRONUÑCIATION
▭	pool	sh (as in spla*sh*!)
◁	hill or slope	qu
⌓	basket	k
⏏	pot/jar stand	g (soft, as in *g*ood)
⌂	loaf of bread	t (as in *t*asty)
⊷	tether rope	ch (as in *ch*ain)
⌔	hand	d
⌇	cobra	j (as in *j*umping)

NOT ALWAYS WHAT IT SEEMS

With ideograms the 'picture' and meaning have a direct link, but with phonograms (including those in the alphabet you've just seen) the pictures and meaning have absolutely nothing to do with each other. It's easy to get confused. That's part of the reason why so many brainy experts failed to crack the 'hieroglyphs code' in the last century.

The phonograms that sound out the word 'zen', for example, are written using the door bolt and waves of water glyphs, like this:

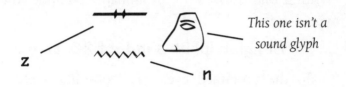

This one isn't a sound glyph

but the word has nothing to do with door bolts or water. It means to kiss.

What, no vowels?

Having just read some vowel sounds in the pronunciation columns of the alphabet, you might be surprised to learn that the Ancient Egyptians didn't actually use vowels when writing in hieroglyphs. (There's no 'e' glyph in 'zen', above, for example.)

Remember, in the 'core alphabet', these are sounds which have been given to the glyphs by *modern day experts*. We don't know for sure how they were really pronounced. What we do know is that the Ancient Egyptians would have spoken with vowel sounds but they didn't bother to record their vowels in their writing.

The reason why experts have given some glyphs vowel sounds is to make it easier for us non-Ancient Egyptians to pronounce them.

The easiest way to imagine how it really was in

Ancient Egyptian times is to think of an English equivalent. If I'm talking, I might say 'The English alphabet is made up of 26 letters' but, if you were writing that down with an alphabet without vowels you'd write:

Th nglsh lphbt s md p f 26 lttrs

To the untrained eye, this looks like gibberish. Even the most simple sentences look like an uncrackable code. 'The elephant sat on the cat on the mat' becomes **Th lphnt st n th ct n th mt**.

But here's the real problem. Trying to fit the right vowels sounds isn't as easy as you might think. Does 'ct' mean acute, cat, coat, cot, coot or cute? Is 'n' an, in, on, ion or one? You see the problem? Even a one-glyph word could have many different meanings. Try working out what these vowelless words say:

1. **N, TW, THR, FR, FV, SX, SVN**

   (CLUE: I'm counting on you.)

2. **STTCH N TM SVS NN**

   (CLUE: a proverb you'll get in time.)

3. **TH HRGLPHS HNDBK**

   (CLUE: an excellent book!)

Answers are on page 94

⌒ A DETERMINED SOLUTION

To get around the problem of having a number of completely different words represented by the same glyphs, the Ancient Egyptians came up with a **third** type of glyph to go with ideograms and phonograms. The glyphs in this third type are called determinatives. Determinatives were put at the end of words to determine what those words are about.

THE THREE TYPES OF GLYPH:

Ideograms
'picture glyphs' showing actual objects or actions.

Phonograms
'sound glyphs' making up words.

Determinatives
glyph word-endings giving us clues as to what the words are about.

Used as a determinative, this glyph of the sun is used to end words about the sun, light and time of day.

Once you get the idea of determinatives, they're really very easy to follow. Let's look at the English sentence 'Fred visited London'. Using the Ancient Egyptian approach of not bothering to include the vowels in the written language, it can be written down as:

FRD VSTD LNDN

Now all we have to do is to add some determinatives.

This determinative at the end of a word means that the glyphs before it are about a man.

This determinative, representing a town or city, is a glyph of a crossroads in a circle.

The determinative for walking or going somewhere is the same glyph as the ideogram 'to walk' or 'to run'.

Include them in our sentence and we get:

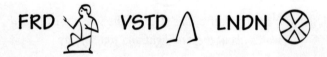

FRD ... VSTD ... LNDN

So, we now know that FRD is a man, VSTD is a 'going' action and that LNDN is a place.

Sometimes, just by looking at the determinative at the end of the word, it's possible to guess what the whole means without having to translate (or 'decode') the other glyphs.

For example, the Ancient Egyptian word *khebi* means to dance. Removing the vowels, it was written

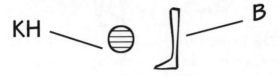

as '*kh*' and '*b*'. You'll see from the alphabet on pages 15 and 16, that these are:

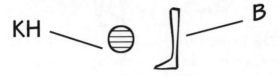

to which was added the determinative of a dancing man, giving us:

Not only is that determinative one great little mover on the dance floor... he's also a very good clue as to what the word means!

Before you read on, guess what this word might mean by looking at the determinative:

Even if you didn't know that the word actually meant 'dog', you probably guessed that it was something to do with an animal.

The same two sound glyphs (which are pronounced 'iew') spell two totally different words – with totally different meanings – when used with two other determinatives as word-endings:

same two
phonograms

different
determinative

This determinative, showing a man with his
hand to his mouth, gives a clue that the word
is something to do with the mouth – speaking, eating,
or some such thing. In this case, the word means
'to show great sadness'.*

yet another
determinative

The same first two glyphs with this third determinative –
of a little sparrow – has yet another different meaning.
The word now means 'evil' or 'wrong'.

DID YOU KNOW?

For some reason, the sparrow glyph was used
to mean small, weak, pathetic... or even evil.
The Ancient Egyptians can't have liked
the poor bird much!

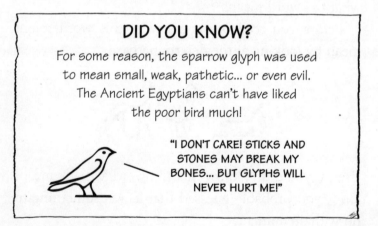

"I DON'T CARE! STICKS AND
STONES MAY BREAK MY
BONES... BUT GLYPHS WILL
NEVER HURT ME!"

On pages 23–25 are some of the most important
determinatives.

*The corners of your mouth turn down when you're sad.

DETERMINATIVES - IMPORTANT CLUES

GLYPH	REPRESENTS	GOES WITH WORDS ABOUT
People and body parts:		
	seated man	types of men, I, me.
	seated woman	types of women.
	beating man	physical actions, such as hitting, attacking.
	upright mummy	mummy, statue, image, picture, shape.
	eye	eye or actions associated with eyes: to look, weep, be awake, be blind.
	eye, nose and cheek	nose, nostrils, to smell, face, joy, pleasure.
	walking legs	to come, go, walk, run, approach, stop, hurry.

23

GLYPH	REPRESENTS	GOES WITH WORDS ABOUT
⟶▷	spit	to spit, vomit, blood.
⬭	gland	illness, death, disease, to embalm.

The Heavens:

✱	star	star, hour, morning, tomorrow.
☉	sun	light and time: sun, day, yesterday, eternity, to rise.
⊏⊐	sky	sky, heaven, high, above, ceiling, gate, to hang.

Objects:

⟍	knife	knife, to slaughter, cut, carve, sharp.

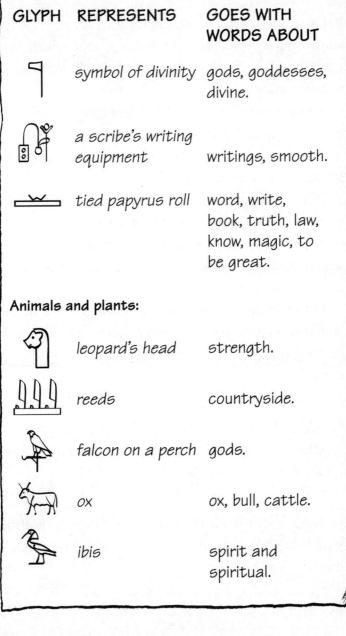

GLYPH	REPRESENTS	GOES WITH WORDS ABOUT
	symbol of divinity	gods, goddesses, divine.
	a scribe's writing equipment	writings, smooth.
	tied papyrus roll	word, write, book, truth, law, know, magic, to be great.

Animals and plants:

GLYPH	REPRESENTS	GOES WITH WORDS ABOUT
	leopard's head	strength.
	reeds	countryside.
	falcon on a perch	gods.
	ox	ox, bull, cattle.
	ibis	spirit and spiritual.

TRANSLITERATION

Before you go any further, here's a quick mention of
something Egyptologists love doing, but which you
won't find in *The Hieroglyphs Handbook*. And that's
transliterating.

Show Egyptologists a wall of hieroglyphs and their
eyes light up and then – before you can say 'I want my
mummy!' they start transliterating left to right, right to
left and top to bottom.

Instead of actually copying down a glyph, if they
want to make a note of it – in other words instead of
trying to draw it – experts use an agreed symbol
which stands for that glyph. This method is called
transliteration.

For example, as you can see from its entry in the
alphabet on page 16, the cobra glyph is pronounced 'j'
(as in 'Jump, you fool! That snake's about to bite your
ankles!').

An eager Egyptologist would transliterate the cobra
glyph to the agreed symbol '<u>d</u>' so:

glyph:	transliteration:	pronunciation:
⌇	<u>**d**</u>	**j**

Because this book is all about reading and writing
actual hieroglyphs, the transliteration ('recording')
stage has been left out. Like the
true Ancient Egyptians before us – well, those few

who could actually read and write, anyway – it's straight to pronunciation and translation! Those Ra-worshipping, pharaoh-praising, pyramid-robbing people didn't transliterate, so why should we?

Rather than write out the Ancient Egyptian word 'to relate' or 'to tell' in glyphs, an Egyptologist might transliterate it into: **sḏd**.

It's much more fun to have a go at writing the actual glyphs yourself. That's what this book is all about. I drew these myself. You could practise by tracing some of the glyphs from the back of the book.

WHERE TO START

So now you know about the three different types of glyphs, you've seen the core alphabet and you've heard about transliteration. What more do you need to know before really getting started? Well, where to start – literally – would be useful.

In English, we read words and sentences from left to right. In Arabic and Hebrew, people read from right to left. In Chinese, people read from top to bottom. In Ancient Egyptian, you can do all three.

Yes, that's right. A string of hieroglyphs can be read from left to right, right to left or top to bottom... So how do you know where to start reading that inscription on a tomb or ancient curse? Where is the beginning of a word or sentence?

When hieroglyphs are written horizontally – side to side, not downwards – there's a simple trick of telling whether you should start reading them from the left or right hand end. Look and see in which directions the people, body parts and animals are facing. If they're facing left, then start reading from the left (as we do in English). That's the way most of the glyphs have been shown in the book so far.

"I THINK IT SAYS THERE'S BEEN A TERRIBLE ACCIDENT!"

If the glyphs are facing right, then start reading from the right. People, body parts and animals always face the direction of the start of a sentence. (So do all the other glyphs, but it's not so easy to tell which way is which with them.) When it comes to writing top to bottom, it doesn't matter if the glyphs face right or left, so long as they all face the same way within a column of text.

Here is the same word, meaning 'answer' written in four different ways:

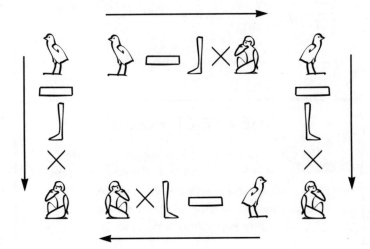

Can you work out which direction the following words should be read in?

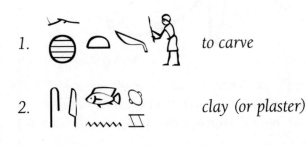

1.   to carve

2.   clay (or plaster)

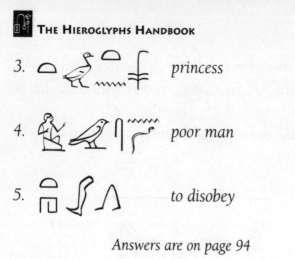

3. princess

4. poor man

5. to disobey

Answers are on page 94

THE EYE OF HORUS

The eye of Horus — also known as the wadjet eye — is a symbol of good luck. Painted on boats, doors and even worn as jewellery, it was said to bring protection to everyone and everything around it.

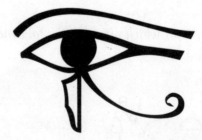

According to myth, the god Horus's eye was ripped out by his uncle, but returned to him by his wife, the goddess Hathor.

"WHY DO YOU KEEP CALLING DADDY A MUMMY?"

THE NAME GAME

Now you're just about ready to write your own name in Ancient Egyptian, in whatever direction you want! Use the letters from the 'core alphabet' on pages 15 and 16 but, first, here are some useful tips.

REMEMBER: this is a sound alphabet, so – if your name has a 'p' and an 'h' in it, making a 'f' sound, choose the 'f' glyph ( ) in the first place. 'Sound out' your name.

BUT: because there's no 'th' sound in Ancient Egyptian, you're going to have to pretend that the 't' glyph ( ) and the 'h' glyph ( ) go together to make 'th'. You'll seem so brainy when you write in hieroglyphs, no one will suspect a thing!

THE MISSING 'L': There's no 'l' sound glyph in the 'alphabet', though some people cheat and say that the ⬭ glyph can be used as an 'l' as well as an 'r'... but remember that this 'alphabet' is only made up of the most regularly used sound glyphs.

Why not use the 'l' that Cleopatra used in her name? If it's good enough for Cleopatra, it's good enough for the rest of us... and if you don't know who Cleopatra was, have a look at page 84).

The 'l' she used was a lion:

I spell my first name, Philip, in Ancient Egyptian hieroglyphs like this:

F   I   L   I   P

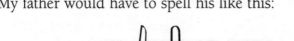

My father would have to spell his like this:

K   R   I   S   T   F   R

You guessed it, it's Christopher.

> **NOTE:** men and boys put the 'man' determinative after their names  and women and girls the 'woman' determinative: .

NAME IN THE FRAME

This leaves one last thing — well, *two* really, to make your name look as authentically Ancient Egyptian as possible. The first of these is the cartouche. The cartouche, which is pronounced 'car-toosh', is a kind of frame which was put around the names of pharaohs. (Okay, so you're not actually an Ancient Egyptian pharaoh, but I won't tell if you won't.) For that reason, cartouches are sometimes known as 'royal rings'. (You can find out more about pharaohs' names on page 38.) They were originally based on a coil of rope, so the name 'Philip' would look something like this:

The glyphs spell out 'FILIP', the determinative tells us that 'FILIP' is a man or a boy's name and the cartouche makes the name stand out from any writing we might put around it.

But notice how the letters have been grouped together to fill the space. This is the last BIG THING you need to remember when reading and writing like an Ancient Egyptian. You've got to...

...THINK LIKE A SCRIBE

As well as making offerings to gods, recording events in history, retelling myths and legends and telling us the purposes of buildings and monuments, hieroglyphs were also designed to look beautiful. It was up to the scribes to make sure that every inch of papyrus or stone looked great... and gappiness does not equal good. Probably one of the very first lessons a would-be scribe learnt was:

GAPPINESS = GOOD ✗
GAPPINESS = BAD ✓

This meant that glyphs in words were grouped together – sometimes some on top of others – to fill the space. If you look back through this book, you'll see that many of the hieroglyphic words you've already met are shown with their glyphs grouped in this way.

You still want people to read the glyphs of a word in a particular order, so there are some oh-so-simple rules to follow.

This is the word 'to complain'. From the way the determinative is facing, we know to start reading from the left, so the reading order would be:

The same word, written to be read from right to left, would be read like this:

Which leaves top to bottom:

Of course, another scribe may choose to group the glyphs in a slightly different way, but the same rules still apply.

GO FOR IT!

Now you should be 100% ready to have a go writing your own name – or names – in all different directions. Good luck!

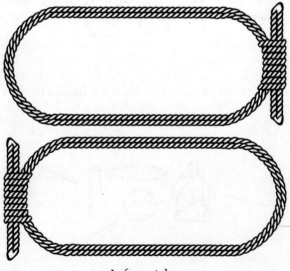

Left to right

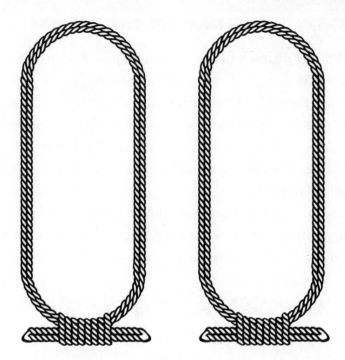

Right to left

You could trace off the glyphs you need from the alphabet (on pages 15 and 16) or you could simply copy them. There's no need to be exact. The glyphs in this book would have been carved, written and painted in many different styles.

DID YOU KNOW?

Scribes were often let off paying taxes
and didn't have to work in the fields,
in return for their writing.

IN THE NAME OF THE KING

When a pharaoh became a pharaoh he was given five 'great names'. The two most important types of name have, themselves, been given names by Egyptologists: the *prenomen* and the *nomen*, or 'coronation name' and 'family name'. These terms would have meant nothing to the Ancient Egyptians, but experts love giving things names.

The Ancient Egyptians didn't call cartouches or royal rings cartouches *or* royal rings. Their name for a cartouche was 'shenu', which was written like this:

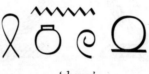

'shenu'

and it was inside two cartouches that the *prenomen* and *nomen* were written.

Here are the pharaoh Tutankhamun's *prenomen* and *nomen*.

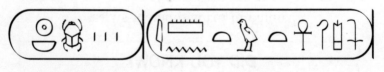

prenomen   *nomen*

A number of important titles went before each cartouche and the same titles were used for thousands of years. This means that if you see photographs of carved Egyptian monuments in books, go to the Egyptology department of a museum or – if you're really lucky – visit some of the ancient sites in Egypt, you're likely to spot at least some of these particular hieroglyphs AND WILL BE ABLE TO TELL YOUR FAMILY AND FRIENDS EXACTLY WHAT THEY MEAN! Will they be impressed? Did the Ancient Egyptians build pyramids?

LOOK OUT FOR:

BEFORE the *prenomen*:

good god

lord of the two lands

King of Upper and
Lower Egypt

BEFORE the *nomen*:

Son of Ra

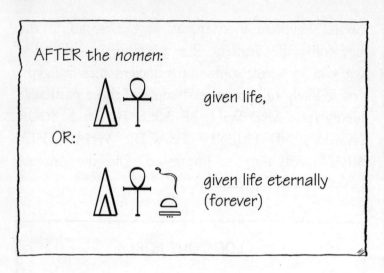

AFTER the *nomen*:

given life,

OR:

given life eternally
(forever)

The hieroglyphs for the word 'king' itself are:

Let's look more closely at the determinative:

*Kings and pharaohs
wore ritual false beards.*

*The beard was a symbol of
kingship. It appeared in paintings,
carvings and even the sarcophagi
of pharaohs.*

*Even ruling queens
had fake beards for
special occasions!*

In fact, kings didn't really get to be called 'pharaohs' until the time of the Middle Kingdom. The word for 'pharaoh' is shown as ⌐ and actually means 'great house'. Here are all the titles put together as they often appear on monuments. You could, of course, add your own first and last names in the cartouches!

good god	lord of the two lands	King of Upper and Lower Egypt	[Prenomen]

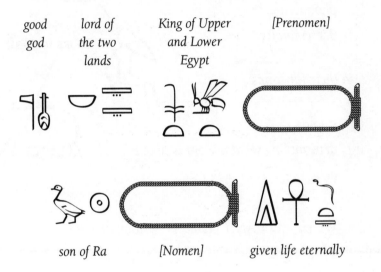

son of Ra   [Nomen]   given life eternally

41

HOW ARE YOU DOING?

It's amazing how much you've probably learnt so far without even realising it. See what you can remember.

1. *Match these types of glyph...*

a. *ideogram*

b. *phonogram*

c. *determinative*

"WAIT! I KNOW THESE!"

"SURE YOU DO..."

...to their functions:

(i) *sounds*

(ii) *determining what a word is about*

(iii) *actual objects or actions*

2. *Which way CAN'T glyphs be written or read:*

a. *left to right,*

b. *right to left,*

c. *top to bottom, or*

d. *bottom to top?*

3. *Do 'body part' glyphs face:*

a. *in the direction we should read, or*

b. *in the direction we should start reading from?*

4. If Ancient Egyptians didn't write down vowels, why do some of the glyphs in the alphabet have vowel sounds?

a. because modern day experts have given them these sounds to make pronunciation easier, or

b. because vowels meant something different in Ancient Egypt?

5. Which of these glyphs is the determinative for 'evil' or 'wrongdoing'?

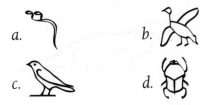

a.   b.

c.   d.

6. What order should the glyphs in the following words be read:

a.   b.

war-cry   *weep*

c.   d.

cut off   *victory*

43

7. Is a 'cartouche':

a. something a scribe keeps his inks in,

b. a word with more than one meaning, or

c. a frame around a name?

8. Amongst these glyphs:

(i)

(ii)

(iii)

(iv)

"THEY'RE IN FOR A
SHOCK WHEN THEY
TURN ROUND!"

find the one which:

a. goes after a man or boy's name,

b. goes after a woman or girl's name, and

c. means a king?

9. Using the 'alphabet', guess how the following word
    (meaning 'great' or 'large') might be pronounced:

determinative

Answers on page 94

"AND THEY CALL THIS A POCKET CALCULATOR?!"

NUMBERS AND NOUNS

You've already been introduced to a few Ancient Egyptian number glyphs in the early pages of *The Hieroglyphs Handbook*, and they're even easier to use than ordinary glyphs.

The basic numerals:		
|	1	stroke/line
∩	10	cattle hobble*
ℓ	100	piece of rope
𓋹	1,000	lotus flower
𓂀	10,000	human finger
𓆐	100,000	tadpole/pollywog
𓁨	1,000,000	a god holding up the sky

*It's what they put around a cow's leg to stop it running away.

45

Once you know these numbers, you can make up all the other numbers in between.

The number 5, for example, is simply five 1s (IIIII). The number 30 is simply three 10 glyphs (∩∩∩), because 3 x 10 = 30. So what would 35 be? The three 10s and 5 ones together, with the bigger numbers going first: ∩∩∩IIIII.

As with other glyphs, numbers can be read left to right, right to left, and up and down, so can 'face' in different directions. They can also be grouped together to take up less space and look more beautiful. And that, in less than two pages, is all you need to know to read and write Ancient Egyptian hieroglyphic numbers!

WHAT ARE THESE NUMBERS?

1.
$$\begin{array}{c} III \\ \cap \ III \\ III \end{array}$$

(Tutankhamun's probable age when he died)

2.
$$\begin{array}{l} \text{⸙} \text{℘} \text{℘} \text{℘} \cap \cap \cap \ III \\ \text{⸙} \text{℘} \text{℘} \text{℘} \cap \cap \cap \ III \\ \text{⸙} \text{℘} \text{℘} \text{℘} \cap \cap \cap \ III \end{array}$$

(Clue: The year The Hieroglyphs Handbook *was first published)*

"I'M A BIRD-BRAIN WHEN IT
COMES TO MATHS!"

3.   ∩∩∩|||
      ∩∩∩||| |

(Years Ramesses II ruled Egypt)

The Ancient Egyptians didn't use '+' and '-' signs, but that's not to stop you having a go at these sums!

4.   ∩∩∩∩||| ∩ ∩ ||
      ∩∩∩∩||| | − ∩ ∩ ||| = **?**
                      ∩ ∩ ||

(Clue: a nice round number)

5. ||𝕀𝟋ℙℙℙ ℙ ∩∩| ℙ∩∩||
      ||𝕀𝟋ℙℙℙℙℙ ∩∩| + ℙ∩ ∩|| = **?**

(No clue!)

6. Now try writing these numbers (left to right) using hieroglyphs:

a. 12   b. 128   c. 1,100,500

Answers on page 94

DID YOU KNOW?

It was the ancient Egyptians
who created the
365 (ℙℙℙ∩∩∩∩∩∩|||||) day year.
They discovered five (|||||) planets in
our solar system.

PLURALS, GENDERS AND DUALS

When we want to write about more than one thing in English it's often simply a matter of putting an 's' on the end of the word. House becomes houses, servant becomes servants and tree becomes trees.

In Ancient Egyptian, a common way of showing that you were writing about more than one thing – making the noun a plural – was to repeat the glyphs, thus:

⌐⌐ = house

⌐⌐ ⌐⌐ = two houses

⌐⌐ ⌐⌐ ⌐⌐ = houses (any number more than two)

or, with more complicated words, simply to repeat the determinatives at the end:

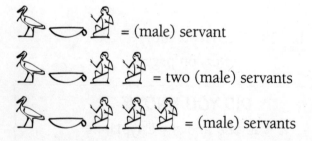

As in languages such as French, Ancient Egyptian words were given a 'gender'. There was no 'it'. They are either masculine (male) or feminine (female) words.

Masculine words have no special ending, but feminine words end in ⌒ (which you may, or may not, remember is pronounced 't'). In the plural, a 𓆇 is sometimes added. (In the case of a feminine word, the 𓆇 is put before the ⌒ so that the word still ends with ⌒ and can be clearly identified as being feminine.)

Look, for example, at the feminine word for 'tree':

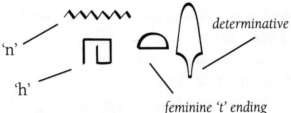

'n'

'h'

determinative

feminine 't' ending

In early Ancient Egyptian hieroglyphic writing, the plural 'trees' would be shown as:

plural ending 'w'

followed by feminine 't' ending

followed by repeated determinative

Over time, someone realised that repeating the glyphs was rather a long-winded way of going about things. It took up a lot of space and was very time consuming. It's important to remember that these weren't words being jotted down with a felt-tip pen on a piece of paper. More often than not, someone was having to chisel them into solid rock or stone... and everything had to fit!

So, eventually, a special plural determinative was created which was made up of three widely spaced ' | ' glyphs, like this: | | | .

Under this new system, the plurals of 'house', 'servant' and 'tree' became:

houses   (male) servants   trees

Notice that the 🐦 glyph has been left out of the masculine plurals when written down.

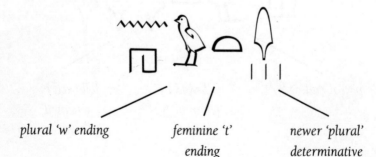

plural 'w' ending   feminine 't'   newer 'plural'
                          ending   determinative

Now here comes the important part. If you want to write down a specific number of items in Ancient Egyptian hieroglyphs, you usually leave the word in the singular and then put the number on the end.

For example, an Ancient Egyptian would write TEN TREES as 'TREE TEN', but in glyphs, of course, so it would look like this:

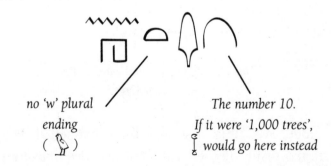

no 'w' plural ending

The number 10. If it were '1,000 trees', would go here instead

If he wanted to write about three or more trees in general, but not be specific, he'd write it as it appears at the bottom of page 49. But what about TWO trees?

51

Unlike English, the Ancient Egyptians didn't only have singulars ('sister') and plurals ('sisters') but also something called duals – special words for when there's just two of something ('a pair of sisters').

To begin with, the idea of repeating the determinative remained, so for two trees, we have the ending ⵕⵕ, for two male servants we have 𓀀𓀀, for two female servants we have 𓁐𓁐. Then, instead of the dual determinatives, a new symbol was introduced to replace them (in the same way that | | | replaced the three determinatives for the plurals). This was: \\, pronounced 'y'.*

This was the masculine dual word ending, pronounced 'wy'.

This was the female dual word ending, pronounced 'ty'.

But, over time, a strange thing happened. People started using the ' \\ ' *and the double determinatives as well.* So \\ became little more than a phonogram (sound glyph) on the end of the word. As a result

* ⵕⵕ is pronounced 'y' too.

many dual words are spelled in a number of different ways.

OH, BROTHER!

To make the word 'brother' into the dual word, meaning two brothers, the glyphs were rearranged and a second determinative was added: . Later, the two determinatives were dropped and replaced with the [shorthand] dual masculine ending of to create: . Then, amazingly, the two determinatives were reintroduced... so, rather than being a shorthand, the final dual word was much longer than the original. It became:

Using all this new-found knowledge, let's turn 'male servant' (singular) into 'female servant' then 'female servants' (plural) and, finally, into 'a pair of female servants' (dual).

We start with 'male servant' (from page 48):

male servant

When changing it to 'female servant', we need to add the feminine ending ⌒ and the feminine determinative 𓁙 , giving us:

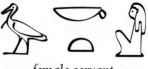

female servant

To turn this into 'female servants' (plural) we now add the glyph 𓅱 to give us the feminine plural ending 𓅱⌒, and add the plural determinative | | | , leaving us with:

female servants

SNEAKY SCRIBE SHORT-CUT

Sometimes scribes left out the 🐦 glyphs in plurals, so you might find 'female servants' written as, 🐦 ⌣ 𓀾 ||| but it's always best to put it in when writing Ancient Egyptian yourself. (It makes you appear to be even more brainy!)

Now to write 'a pair of female servants'. We need to look at the single 'female servant' and add the \\ glyph after the ⌣ to give us the feminine dual ending pronounced 'ty'. Then all we have to do is add a second woman determinative, leaving us with:

a pair of female servants

REMEMBER: If we want to write about a specific number of servants, we simply use the singular spelling of the word, and add the number after the determinative:

232 male servants

1,100 female servants

See if you can create the plural and duals of the following animals. (Watch out for those feminine endings):

1. Cobra

2. Crocodile

3. Pig

4. Duck

Answers on page 94

56

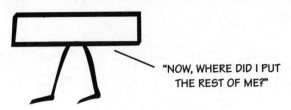

"NOW, WHERE DID I PUT THE REST OF ME?"

PUTTING IT ALL TOGETHER

All being well (with the gods on your side), you should have a pretty good idea of how to tackle reading and writing hieroglyphs by now. Of course, you'll need a list of useful words to use and you'll find plenty of those in the back of this book, including the words you've already encountered to get this far.

The important thing is to know the order that the words usually go in to make up a sentence. In English, our most basic sentences are subject + verb + object, such as:

THE COBRA
(subject)

HEARS
(verb)

THE PIG
(object)

The Ancient Egyptians – who didn't bother with definite and indefinite articles (that's 'the's and 'a's and 'an's to you and me) – would have written the words in a different order.

Their basic sentences are: *verb + subject + object* so, in this example, THE COBRA HEARS THE PIG would be written as:

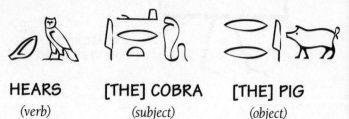

HEARS
(*verb*)

[THE] COBRA
(*subject*)

[THE] PIG
(*object*)

So THE DUCK (*subject*) HEARS (*verb*) THE CROCODILE (*object*) would be written in Ancient Egyptian as HEARS (*verb*) DUCK (*subject*) CROCODILE (*object*), like this:

HEARS
(*verb*)

[THE] DUCK
(*subject*)

[THE] CROCODILE
(*object*)

VERB ENDINGS

Many Ancient Egyptian verbs have a basic form and then a different ending, depending on who is the subject of the sentence – in other words, who is 'doing' the verb.

In sentences where it is used to state 'an objective fact' (such as 'the dog eats the bone'), the verb endings match those of the verb 'to hear':

 I hear

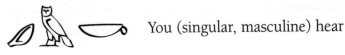 You (singular, masculine) hear

You (singular, feminine) hear

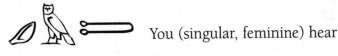 He hears

 She hears

We hear

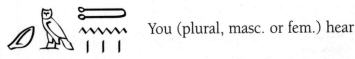 You (plural, masc. or fem.) hear

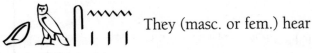 They (masc. or fem.) hear

These verb endings can also be used with nouns (subjects and objects) as pronouns (words which can replace nouns) or possessives (words that tell us who something belongs to).

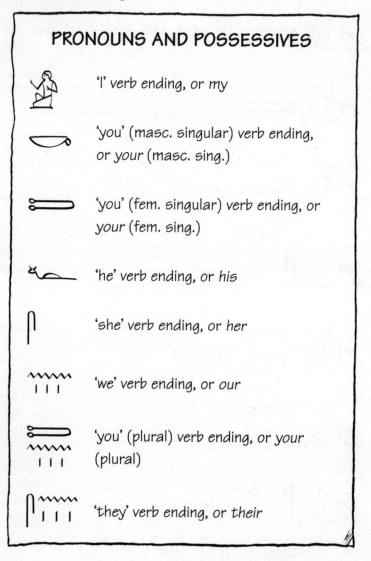

PRONOUNS AND POSSESSIVES

'I' verb ending, or *my*

'you' (masc. singular) verb ending, or *your* (masc. sing.)

'you' (fem. singular) verb ending, or *your* (fem. sing.)

'he' verb ending, or *his*

'she' verb ending, or *her*

'we' verb ending, or *our*

'you' (plural) verb ending, or *your* (plural)

'they' verb ending, or *their*

So 'my town' would become 'town' ⊗ with 'my' 🐦 on the end, like this: ⊗ 🐦 'Her house' would be 'house' ⊏⊐ with 'her' 𓏭 on the end: ⊏⊐ 𓏭.

ON AND ON...

Other very useful words, that keep cropping up in ancient hieroglyphs, and which are equally useful when you're writing messages yourself, are the prepositions (in, on, to, with, from, etc.).

Here are the most common ones but, like most of Ancient Egyptian, there are usually variations – in other words, more than one word with the same meaning.

as well as being the 'm' phonogram in the 'core alphabet', the owl also means *in, from* or *with*

as well as being the 'n' phonogram, this glyph also means *to, of* or *for.*

as well as being the 'r' phonogram, this glyph also means *to* (an alternative to above) or *towards.*

means *on.*

means *with* or *near.*

means *under.*

61

There is no hard and fast rule where they go, though they usually appear near the end of a sentence and often immediately before the object, such as:

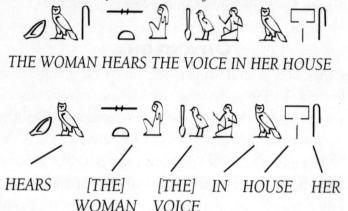

THE WOMAN HEARS THE VOICE IN HER HOUSE

| *HEARS* | *[THE] WOMAN* | *[THE] VOICE* | *IN* | *HOUSE* | *HER* |

WHAT, NO VERB?

In certain cases, the verb is left out of a sentence altogether. Egyptologists used to call these 'non-verbal' sentences – if you read the hieroglyphs out loud, the sentences didn't make sense, for example:

(MALE) SLAVES IN HOUSE

actually means THE SLAVES ARE IN THE HOUSE. Like the missing 'the's, 'a's and 'an's, when reading a non-verbal sentence, the reader has to know to add the verb – in this case, the 'ARE'.

AND ANOTHER THING!

The Ancient Egyptians never wrote down 'and's either. They would simply run two words together.

For example, as has been said before, gods and goddesses played a very important part in the lives of the Ancient Egyptians – at least worshipping them did.

The word 'god' is ' ⸢⸣| ' and 'gods' is ' ⸢⸣|| '. The three strokes, one on top of the other, are simply a variation of the plural determinative '| | |'. Scribes chose to write them one on top of the other because they go well with the tall, thin glyph – it's space-saving and looks pretty, which (I hope you know by now) were two important factors in a scribe's work.

The word 'goddess' is:

so, following the rules discussed in the last chapter, 'goddesses' should be:

In fact, scribes soon used shorthand again, and turned it into:

63

Put the two words together without a glyph in between:

and 'gods/goddesses' miraculously becomes 'gods AND goddesses'.

So 'The gods and goddesses hear the praise' would be written as: *HEAR GODS GODDESSES PRAISE* which, in hieroglyphs, reads as:

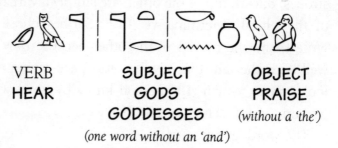

VERB	SUBJECT	OBJECT
HEAR	**GODS**	**PRAISE**
	GODDESSES	*(without a 'the')*
	(one word without an 'and')	

HAVE A GO!

Using all this information, have a go at writing the following sentences and phrases in hieroglyphs. Any words you'll need (which you haven't been introduced to already) are in the box on page 65:

1. IN MY HOUSE

2. BROTHER AND SISTER

3. THE SCRIBE WRITES A LETTER

4. THE GOAT EATS GRAPES

5. THE HERDSMAN SHOOTS AN ARROW

ARROW

LETTER

EAT[S]

SCRIBE

GOAT

SHOOT[S]

GRAPES

SISTER

HERDSMAN

WRITE[S]

"DON'T WORRY. I'M NOT DEAD. THIS IS JUST A LIE-DOWN PROTEST UNTIL HE MENTIONS HIPPOS ALONG WITH ALL THE OTHER ANIMALS!"

"MIND IF I JOIN YOU?"

ADJECTIVES

In Ancient Egyptian, adjectives – words which describe nouns – go immediately after the person or things they're describing, and match their gender. In other words, if the noun has a feminine ending, the adjective it's describing has one too.

Adjectives are also supposed to match the noun if it's plural or dual but scribes rarely bothered with this, which is why it's unusual to find adjectives with plural or dual endings. (Hieroglyphs took such a long time to write, and took up such a lot of space, that such short cuts make perfect sense.)

To be authentically Ancient Egyptian, then, I suggest you ignore plural and dual endings when you're writing hieroglyphic adjectives.

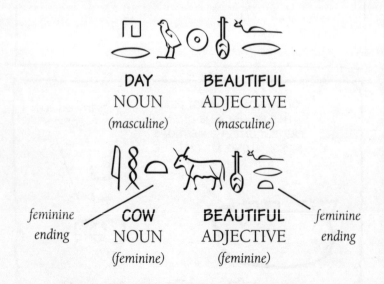

DAY
NOUN
(*masculine*)

BEAUTIFUL
ADJECTIVE
(*masculine*)

feminine ending

COW
NOUN
(*feminine*)

BEAUTIFUL
ADJECTIVE
(*feminine*)

feminine ending

CATTLE
NOUN
*(plural
feminine)*

BEAUTIFUL
ADJECTIVE
*(feminine, but no
plural ending)*

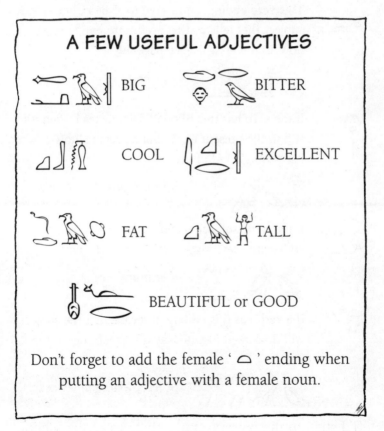

A FEW USEFUL ADJECTIVES

BIG

BITTER

COOL

EXCELLENT

FAT

TALL

BEAUTIFUL or GOOD

Don't forget to add the female ' ⌒ ' ending when
putting an adjective with a female noun.

PAST, PRESENT AND FUTURE

Writing different tenses in Ancient Egyptian hieroglyphs is very complicated, because different types of verbs behave in different ways... and one thing harder than using the different tenses is trying to explain them. It gives me a headache and makes me grumpy. Here are a few clues on what to look out for:

 This verb ending, connected to a masculine single subject (he) tells us that events are happening now, in the *present*. [See page 59]

 = he hears

If the verb has this BEGINNING instead, then it's still in the present tense, but a specific 'now-happening' kind of present.

 = he is hearing/is listening

If the same subject is connected to a verb that ends with these glyphs, then it's in the *past*.

 = he heard

If a verb has this ending, it means that the subject will do something, or may do something, in the *future*.

= [one] who will/may hear

(I'd stick to the present until you go to scribe school, if I were you!)

THE OFFERING FORMULA

The title of this chapter is 'Putting it all together' but, when reading hieroglyphic inscriptions, it's really a matter of taking it all apart.

One inscription you'll see again and again and again (in much the same way that the various titles of the pharaohs, discussed on pages 38 to 41, are so common) is what is now known by many as the 'offering formula'.

It's written – with small differences – on tomb walls, sarcophagi, here, there and everywhere. You're bound to find it so, if you can learn it, you're guaranteed to leave everyone else well and truly gobsmacked.

The formula usually begins with ⸬⸗ which means 'an offering which the king gives'. Sometimes, though, it begins ⸬⸗ , which means 'an offering which Anubis [the god] gives'. Find either of these, and you're off to a great start. Next comes ⸬⸗ which is 'Osiris' (god of the afterlife), often followed by ⸬⸗ which means 'lord of Busiris' and by ⸬⸗ which means 'lord of Abydos'. (Busiris and Abydos were two towns connected with Osiris.) Now comes an important part, the glyphs ▱ which mean 'so that he may give an offering of bread, and beer', followed by a list of other offerings. These regularly include 🐂 'beef', ◊ 'alabaster' and ⊔⊔ 'linen' (or 'clothing'). Next comes ⌣ meaning 'for the ka [spirit] of', followed by the name of the person the offering is for. Put it together and, in a typical example, you get:

An offering which the king gives to Osiris, lord of Busiris and lord of Abydos,

so that he may give an offering of bread and beef, alabaster and linen for the spirit of

the mistress of the house, [Suzy.] *

*Only in this example, of course!

"WAIT A MINUTE!
ARE YOU EVER
GOING TO GIVE US
THE GLYPHS FOR
'HIPPO'?"

OVER TO YOU

By now, you've been given the basics of one of the oldest written languages in the world. You've been shown the core alphabet, found out the jobs of the three different types of glyphs, been given the most important determinatives, shown what goes where in a sentence... as well as what to look out for on Ancient Egyptian inscriptions.

Now it's over to you. Over the next few pages you can read all about how – less than 200 years ago – the secret of the hieroglyphs was revealed, and how and why written languages came into being in the first place. But when it comes to writing messages in hieroglyphs, that's down to you. It's a lot of fun! Good luck.

You'll find a list of useful hieroglyphic words and phrases on pages 88 to 91.

CRACKING THE CODE

We haven't always known how to read Ancient Egyptian hieroglyphs – the secret was lost for over a thousand years – and it took an amazing amount of research and detective work to crack the 'code'.

The big break came when a group of Napoleon's soldiers discovered a stone slab covered in writing near a town called Rashid in Egypt, in 1799.

The slab is known today as the Rosetta Stone, after the old name for the town. The slab, made of grey granitoid with pink veins, was covered in writing. It must have been part of a stela (or commemorative plaque) from an Ancient Egyptian temple and dates from 196 BC.

What made the Rosetta Stone such an unbelievably fantastic discovery is that it was covered in three different types of writing: hieroglyphic at the top, demotic (another Egyptian script) in the middle and Greek at the bottom.

It seemed likely that each type of writing was spelling out the same message. In other words, each script was a translation of the others... and people knew how to read Greek, so they would know what the hieroglyphs were supposed to say. Now all they had to do was break the language down and work out exactly what each glyph meant. This was, of course, much easier said than done.

After Napoleon was defeated by the British, the stone was shipped to England and, in 1802, it was put in the British Museum where it's still on display today. But it is thanks to one of Napoleon's countrymen – a Frenchman called Jean-François Champollion – that you now have *The Hieroglyphs Handbook* in your hand. It was this brilliantly brainy young man who cracked the code.

THE EXPERTS' BIG MISTAKES

The problems that all the experts had in trying to crack the code of these Ancient Egyptian hieroglyphs was that they wrongly assumed that all the glyphs were ideograms (picture glyphs). They had no idea that some of the glyphs were phonograms, used to sound out the

"IT MUST BE SOMETHING TO DO WITH A BIRD EATING A MAN'S LEG!"

words, or that others were determinatives giving an important clue as to what the words were about. They thought that each and every glyph was a picture word.

Because they had this idea in their minds before they'd even started to try to crack the code, all the experts ended up in the same place: nowhere.

THE YOUNG ONE

Then, an Englishman called Thomas Young made an important connection. He realised that some of the letters in the demotic script – the writing sandwiched between the hieroglyphic and Greek scripts on the Rosetta Stone – looked very like some of the Ancient Egyptian glyphs.

An idea began to form in his mind: What if the demotic letters had developed out of the glyphs? What if they were simplified squiggles of these pictures? If that was the case, then surely these glyphs would have to be *letters*, not picture words, too?

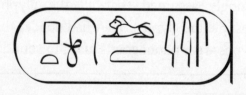

From what he'd read in the Greek script, Young believed that this cartouche (which appears on the Rosetta Stone three times) sounded out the name Ptolemy.

It was like finding a really important missing piece of a jigsaw puzzle down the back of the sofa while everyone else was looking for it under the table – but this was no ordinary jigsaw because, once completed, it would open up a whole new world, revealing the secrets of an amazing ancient civilization!

THE RESEARCH GOES ON

Sadly, Young soon decided that just a few of the glyphs were 'sound letters' and that these were probably only used for special words, such as foreign names which couldn't easily be written in Ancient Egyptian. Nearly all the other glyphs, he decided, were symbolic picture glyphs. He printed the results of his work in 1819.

This was the Ancient Egyptians' own word for 'hieroglyphs'.
It means 'writing of the divine words'.

THE BIG BREAKTHROUGH

Jean-François Champollion made a more thorough investigation. An obelisk removed from Aswan included two cartouches and, written on the base in Greek, were the names Ptolemy and Cleopatra. When Champollion received a copy of these cartouches, he checked one against the cartouche identified on the Rosetta Stone as being Ptolemy's. They matched.

Excitedly, Champollion managed to translate the cartouches. Once this was done, he had successfully identified twelve glyphs which he could then use to begin to translate other cartouches and even words and sentences.

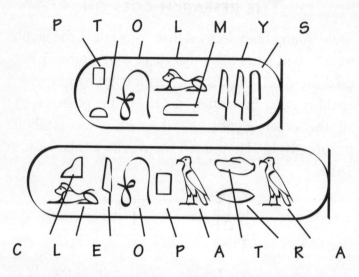

When translating the two names, Champollion discovered that the letter 't' was represented by 'Ω' in the first and 'O' in the second. He realised that, in some cases, different signs could (sometimes) represent the same sound.

The next cartouche he tried contained six glyphs he'd already identified from the first two so – once again like a jigsaw puzzle – he had to try and fill in the blanks.

A   L   ?   S   E   ?   T   R   ?

*Champollion was quick to realise that this must be the
name of the famous ruler and general Alexander, spelt
Alksentrs. Adding the 'k', 'n' and alternative 's', he
now knew even more phonograms.*

Soon, Champollion was finding it easier and easier to translate cartouche after cartouche, as his 'alphabet' grew bigger and bigger. He published his first findings in 1822.

It was in 1824 that he published *Précis du Système Hiéroglyphique* and revealed his startling conclusion: that the phonograms (sound glyphs) were the heart and soul of the hieroglyphic script, supported by ideograms (picture glyphs) and determinatives. He included the translations of many names, words, phrases and sentences and even gave examples of grammar.

More work needed to be done before hieroglyphs could be understood in the way that they are today, but Jean-François Champollion was the first person to read hieroglyphs in over 1,500 years. He was also the founder of modern Egyptology.

"CONGRATULATIONS!
YOU'RE NOW THE
PROUD MUMMY OF A
HEALTHY BABY NOUN!"

THE BIRTH OF WRITING

Nowadays, it's obvious what writing is for. You only have to write something once and, because the words can be copied, lots of different people can read what you have to say. In the days before writing, if a person had something to say, he had to say it out loud. If he wanted different people to hear his story or message again, he had to repeat it, or hope other people would pass it on – through speech. Either way, spoken messages were likely to change as they were passed on.

Have you ever played the game of Chinese Whispers, where a whole group of you stand in a row and whisper a message from one to the other, all the way down the row? More often than not, the message comes out very different at the end.

A famous example of this is an urgent message sent across a battlefield.

It starts out as:

> **"Enemy advancing on left flank!**
> **Please send reinforcements!"**

and ends up as:

> **"Enemy dancing on wet plank!**
> **Please send three or four pence!"**

Writing the message down would avoid the confusion!

THE FIRST PEOPLE

The first humans (it's those early *Homo sapiens sapiens* I first mentioned on page ∩*) were what we call 'hunter gatherers'. They were always out and about – yes, you guessed it – hunting and gathering. (The name was a bit of a giveaway now, wasn't it?) In other words, they were on the lookout for animals to kill, and berries, seeds and roots to gather and eat. There was no need for writing because life was one long search for food. You found it. You ate it. What would anyone have had to write about?

Everyone's diary would have read:

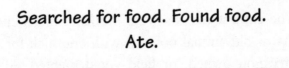

> **Searched for food. Found food.**
> **Ate.**

*10.

79

Or, if he was unlucky:

> ### Searched for food. Didn't find any.
> ### Still searching.

Then the time came when humans invented farming. Today, it's hard to imagine that farming had to be invented. We think of microchips and lasers as inventions, not growing crops and looking after animals. But the idea of farming was an amazing advance.

Suddenly, people weren't out and about and forever on the move. They were growing their own crops and raising their own animals. They could settle down and create real communities. Now, with lots of people in one place, it was necessary to know what belonged to whom. At last, there was a need for keeping written records.

These hieroglyphs make up the word 'to plough'

The earliest records were probably nicks cut into sticks or old animal bones – with one nick for every animal you owned, or field you'd planted. All very simple. All very useful.

NUMBER ONE SUN

Another important use for writing, for early humans, was religion. People were strong believers that the world around them was controlled by different gods or spirits. How else could you explain thunder, or that big, orange ball burning up in the sky every day? Many words and messages in early writing were written in praise of such gods.

A scarab   *'ra', meaning 'sun'*   *'Ra', the 'sun god'*

(The different determinatives give them different meanings)

The Ancient Egyptians worshipped the mighty sun god Ra. (So mighty, in fact, that this book is dedicated to him so as not to upset him.) They had many different images of Ra. One was as a scarab, which is also known as a dung beetle. Perhaps it was thought that, like a dung beetle holding a ball of dung, Ra held the orange ball that was the sun in the sky. This would, of course, have been a lot less smelly, but much heavier and hotter.

Ancient Egyptians carved many pointed monuments called obelisks, all covered in hieroglyphs praising their sun god Ra.

SACRED WORDS

The word 'hieroglyph' actually comes from Ancient Greek, rather than Ancient Egyptian. It means 'sacred writing'. Remember, Egyptians began writing in hieroglyphs about 5,000 years ago and were still using them on monuments, temples and official documents 3,500 years later.

That's not to say that the glyphs didn't change over time. Hieroglyphs started out as simple picture writing, but soon developed into the amazing written language we've looked at in this book.

"AND YOU'LL DEVELOP INTO AN AMAZING FROG!"

"THAT'S A RELIEF. I WAS WONDERING WHAT I WAS SUPPOSED TO BE."

ANCIENT EGYPT

The people of Ancient Egypt didn't speak the same language for the thousands of years of their remarkable civilisation. It changed and developed over time. No one seems to agree on the exact dates (c. means 'about'), but here's an idea of how and when the language developed.

ARCHAIC EGYPTIAN was spoken up to c.2650 BC but very little writing survives from this period – a period when Upper and Lower Egypt were first united under one king (with a funny red and white crown) and grew in power and importance.

OLD EGYPTIAN was spoken and written for about 550 years, from c.2650 BC to c.2100 BC – the time of the first pyramids. (By the way, if any one asks you what is the point of a pyramid, say 'the bit at the very top.')

CLASSICAL EGYPTIAN (sometimes called Middle Egyptian) was spoken from c.2100 BC to c.1550 BC – a time of strong rulers, when the capital moved from Memphis to Thebes – but was used as the official written language of Ancient Egypt from then on.

LATE EGYPTIAN was spoken from c.1550 BC and used for less formal writing from c.1350 BC. This is the language Tutankhamun, the boy king, would have used in his short life before he was buried in the Valley of the Kings (only to be dug up about 3,245 years later by Howard Carter and Lord Carnarvon in 1922).

DEMOTIC was written and spoken from c.650 BC.

COPTIC came into use in c.AD 250.

During the period that these last two languages were spoken, the Persians ruled Ancient Egypt, were kicked out and then ruled again. Next came the Macedonian kings (from Macedonia, of course), the Ptolemies (who included the glamorous queen Cleopatra, who used to be dead famous but is now famous and dead) and, finally, the Romans in 30 BC.

SACRED WORDS

Hieroglyphs were first used when Archaic Egyptian was being spoken, and still being written on papyrus and chiselled into stone when Old and Classical Egyptian were the spoken languages of the day.

These four glyphs actually make up the word for 'glyph'
in Ancient Egyptian.

There are only 26 letters in the English alphabet. These 26 letters have to be mixed together to represent over 40 different sounds that we need to use to be able to speak all the different words in the English language – now over 1,000,000 (🏛).

No one ever uses all of these words. You'd probably use up all the free space in your brain trying to remember them, and most English-speaking people get through life with a vocabulary of about 20,000, so there's no need.

It's the same with Ancient Egyptian hieroglyphs. At least 6,000 have been recorded, but – as you should have discovered by now – you need very few to start reading and writing your first sentences.

'zesh', to write.

The final glyph represents a rolled up scroll of papyrus (a kind of paper made from reeds).

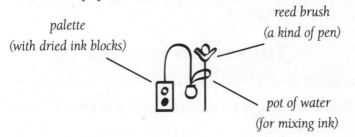

palette
(with dried ink blocks)

reed brush
(a kind of pen)

pot of water
(for mixing ink)

This glyph shows the tools of the scribe's trade.

THE TEXTS

Hieroglyphs had many uses. Papyrus records still survive of court reports telling how robbers broke into royal tombs! Ancient Egyptian myths and legends are also retold in hieroglyphs, so it's possible for us to share stories that were first told by word-of-mouth thousands and thousands of years ago.

One of the most important uses of hieroglyphic writing – at least, as far as the Ancient Egyptians themselves were concerned – was recording the prayers and magic spells that were supposed to help the dead into the next world.

These words were first carved onto the walls of the burial chambers inside pyramids, so Egyptologists now call them the Pyramid Texts.

Later, the spells and prayers were updated – though we're still talking about thousands of years ago – and put on the sides of sarcophagi or coffins. No prizes, then, for guessing why Egyptologists call these the Coffin Texts.

THE BOOK OF THE DEAD

By the time of the New Kingdom, just over three-and-a-half thousand years ago, the spells and prayers were written on papyrus scrolls placed inside the tombs. These scrolls are now referred to as *The Book of the Dead*, though it's not one particular book in the sense that, say, *The Hieroglyphs Handbook* is. According to *The Book of the Dead*, the souls of bad people were eaten by a creature called 'the gobbler' – a job that wouldn't have been to everyone's taste.

(BURP!)

"I MUST HAVE EATEN SOMEONE WHO DISAGREED WITH ME!"

(Fortunately for the gobbler – who called itself 'Amemait' when trying to impress friends – it was part crocodile, part lion and part a few other things, and obviously enjoyed its work.)

MAGIC GLYPHS

There are Ancient Egyptian inscriptions which include animal glyphs whose feet have been left off by the scribe or, in the case of snake glyphs, whose heads have been cut off from their bodies.

It's now thought that the scribes were worried that their sacred writing might have had an inbuilt magic power, somehow allowing these glyphs to come to life.

Without feet, the animals couldn't run away... and decapitated, the snakes could cause no harm!

Superstition obviously changed with time. There are examples of inscriptions where the 'dangerous' glyphs have been defaced and destroyed by later generations, not by the original scribes.

USEFUL WORDS AND PHRASES

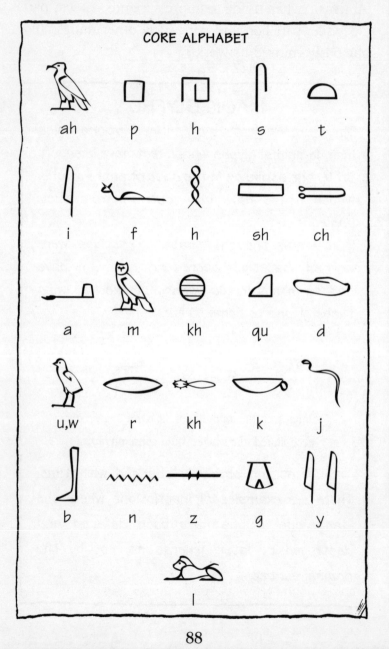

CORE ALPHABET

ah	p	h	s	t
i	f	h	sh	ch
a	m	kh	qu	d
u,w	r	kh	k	j
b	n	z	g	y

l

SOME USEFUL QUESTIONS:

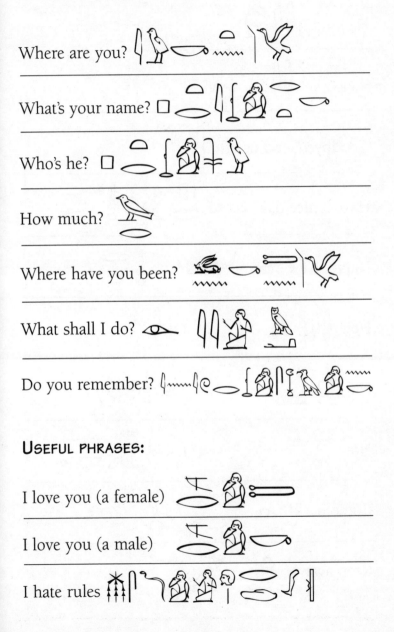

Where are you?

What's your name?

Who's he?

How much?

Where have you been?

What shall I do?

Do you remember?

USEFUL PHRASES:

I love you (a female)

I love you (a male)

I hate rules

89

Hello!

Welcome!

Goodbye/Good health!

Have a nice day!

Happy New Year!

Hey!   O!

Ha!   Yes!

No!   Look!

Come back!

Keep away!

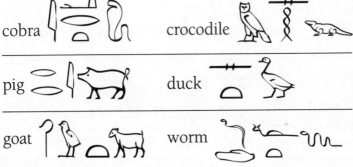

PEOPLE:

mother	us
father	us two
sister	everyone
brother	fool
daughter	friend
enemy	nurse
master of secrets	chief/boss

ANIMALS:

cobra	crocodile
pig	duck
goat	worm

MORE USEFUL WORDS:

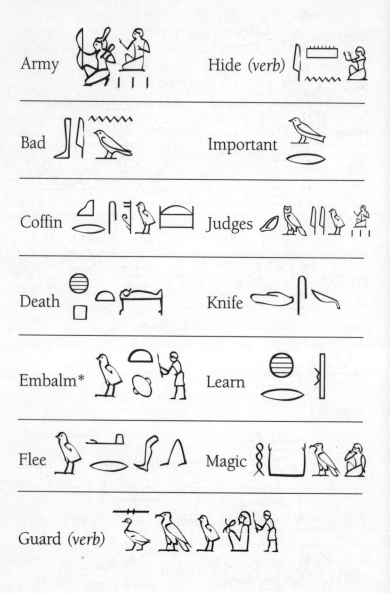

Army

Hide (verb)

Bad

Important

Coffin

Judges

Death

Knife

Embalm*

Learn

Flee

Magic

Guard (verb)

*Make mummies.

Neighbourhood

Outside | Untie

Push | Victory

Recall | Weapons

Sail (*verb*) | Youth

Terror

CALENDAR

Day | Month

Night | Year

Yesterday | Summer

Tomorrow | Winter

Holiday

ANSWERS

PAGE 18

1. ONE, TWO, THREE, FOUR, FIVE, SIX, SEVEN
2. A STITCH IN TIME SAVES NINE
3. THE HIEROGLYPHS HANDBOOK

PAGES 29-30

1. Left to right   2. Left to right   3. Right to left
4. Right to left   5. Left to right

PAGES 42-43

1. a.(iii), b.(i), c.(ii)   2.d.   3.b.   4.a.   5.c.

6. a. ⬜🦉⬜🦉 ...   b. ... 2

c. ... 3   d. ...

7.c. 8.a.(i), b.(iv), c.(iii) 9.'a-aa'

PAGES 46-47

1. 19 2. 1999 3. 67 4. 0 5. 23,000
6. a. ∩ | | b. ∩ | | | | c. ...

PAGE 56

1. plural [...]   dual [...]
2. plural [...]   dual [...]
3. plural [...]   dual [...]
4. plural [...]   dual [...]

PAGE 64

1. [...]   2. [...]   3. [...]
4. [...]
5. [...]

94

BOOKS WORTH A LOOK

Egyptian Grammar, [3rd Edition Revised] by Sir Alan Gardiner, Griffith Institute, Oxford, 1957.*

A Concise Dictionary of Middle Egyptian by R.O. Faulkner, Griffith Institute, Oxford, 1962.*

Egyptian Hieroglyphs, [Reading the Past series] by W.V. Davies, British Museum Press, 1987.

ABC of Egyptian Hieroglyphs by Jaromir Malek, Ashmolean Museum, Oxford, 1994.

How to Read Egyptian Hieroglyphs by Mark Collier & Bill Manley, British Museum Press, 1998.

A Short History of Ancient Egypt by T.G.H. James, Cassell, 1995.

HIPPOPOTAMUS

"BETTER LATE THAN NEVER!"

*Only for the very (clever)!

INDEX